I0804895

IMAGES
of America

ALAMEDA NAVAL AIR STATION

On the Cover: Four Douglas A4D-1s of Attack Squadron 93, the "Blue Blazers," are flying just above the Alameda Naval Air Station runways in early 1957. The Oakland Army Depot is to the right of the Oakland Estuary, San Francisco is in the upper left corner, and Treasure Island is in the upper right just above the San Francisco-Oakland Bay Bridge. Alameda-based VA-93 was the first West Coast squadron to receive these new planes in late 1956, and after further training with them embarked as part of Air Wing Nine on the USS *Ticonderoga* (CVA-14) in September 1957. (Courtesy of the U.S. Navy.)

IMAGES
of America

ALAMEDA NAVAL AIR STATION

William T. Larkins and the
Alameda Naval Air Museum

ARCADIA
PUBLISHING

ISBN 978-0-7385-8040-1

Published by Arcadia Publishing
Charleston, South Carolina

Printed in the United States of America

Library of Congress Control Number: 2009938071

For all general information contact Arcadia Publishing at:
Telephone 843-853-2070
Fax 843-853-0044
E-mail sales@arcadiapublishing.com
For customer service and orders:
Toll-Free 1-888-313-2665

Visit us on the Internet at www.arcadiapublishing.com

This book is dedicated to all the men and women of the military service and the civilian employees who built and maintained one of the largest naval air stations in the United States.

—Marilyn York, President
Alameda Naval Air Museum

Contents

Acknowledgments

Thankful appreciation is due to the following individuals: Barbara Baack, David Balmer, Joseph Baugher, Mark Blackman, Capt. F. James Dodge, Carol Fairweather, Nevins Frankel, Steve Ginter, Deward Gresham, Terry Howell, Buddy Joyce, Steve Kovacs, Pamela Kruse-Buckingham, Richard Lee, Peter Manfre, Robina Masterson, Woody Minor, Lillian Molzan, Fabio Pena, Larry Pirack, Steve Quock, Ronald Reuther, Kin Robles, Richard Rutter, Lawrence Smalley, Gerald Stein, William Stubkjaer, Carol McCann Trotter, Tim Tyler, Nicholas Veronico, Donald Walsh, and Dolly Wilson.

This book would not have been possible without the contributions and patience of Marilyn York, president of the Alameda Naval Air Museum; and Devon Weston, West publisher for Arcadia Publishing.

INTRODUCTION

Though no longer true, the island of Alameda was once the site of many historical aviation events and operations going back to 1910. The land that was eventually obtained by the navy for the Alameda Naval Air Station (NAS Alameda) was originally envisioned in the 1920s as a navy ship facility. In the interim, the Curtiss-Wright Corporation leased land at the west end of the island for one of its national chain of commercial airports. When this was taken over by Pan American Airways it became the world famous home of the Martin 130 "China Clipper."

In 1930, the modern, advanced San Francisco Bay Airdrome opened on Webster Street for both airline and private flying. Described as "one of the great air terminals of the country," it continued until 1940, when it was closed because of future flight interference with the new NAS Alameda.

With the advent of World War II in Europe, military planning was accelerated, and the start of the Army Air Corps Benton Field was interrupted. The navy established a large air station to service the Pacific Fleet. Several years of work preceded the commissioning of NAS Alameda in November 1940. By the time the United States entered the war on December 7, 1941, the air station had become a fully operating base with both patrol plane squadrons and the Overhaul and Operations Department that was later to become its largest tenant.

Thousands of civil service employees worked in this facility between 1941 and 1997 when the air station was closed. They often remember it by the name when they were there, as it went through four changes from Overhaul and Assembly, to Overhaul and Repair, to Naval Air Rework Facility, to Naval Aviation Depot.

Home of many aircraft carriers and squadrons, as well as the overhaul work, NAS Alameda was finally silenced as part of the national presidential order of the Base Realignment and Closure Act. A public ceremony was held in June 1996, and the air station was formally decommissioned in April 1997.

One of the common problems with historical societies and museums is the receipt of unidentified photographs. Well-meaning persons donate historical photographs of families and events, and so on, with no information about the names of the people, the dates that the pictures were taken, or what is depicted in the image and where. In addition, it is unrealistic to expect people to remember names and details from 40 to 50 years ago, particularly when most of them were at Alameda less than 10 years out of the 56 that it was in operation. This is especially true of employees who worked at NAS Alameda during World War II.

This project has been no exception, and a number of photographs have been left out because of this problem, and several will be seen to have incomplete descriptions and a lack of individual identification. We are all guilty of this, but perhaps this reminder will help someone in the future.

Abbreviations for two of the photograph credits are as follows: USN is for U.S. Navy, and WTL is for William T. Larkins.

One

Alameda before the Air Station

Although Pan American Airways may be the best known of the early aviation activities in Alameda, the largest operation was San Francisco Bay Airdrome on Webster Street. Opened in August 1930 and described as "one of the great air terminals of the country" at the time, it had service by Western Air Express, West Coast Air Transport, and Air Ferries, whose amphibians left every 20 minutes for San Francisco. It flourished until 1941, when it was forced to close because of the proximity of its flight operations to the new NAS Alameda. The plane shown is a Consolidated *Fleetster* 20-A being used by the Alameda county sheriff after service at the airport by Condor Airlines. (Deward Gresham.)

A Ranger-powered Fairchild 24R is shown landing to the west over Webster Street. The Webster Street Tube can be seen in the right background. There was a convenient bus stop at the airport and parking for cars behind the fence. San Francisco Bay Airdrome was unique for its rooftop advertising of the airport businesses. (WTL.)

This 1939 aerial view of Alameda Airport looking northwest shows how close it was to the Oakland Estuary at an altitude of only 10 feet. Southern Pacific electric commute trains leading to the Alameda Pier ferryboats ran alongside the airport. Rated as a commercial airport in 1932, it had a 2,500-foot oiled and sand-surfaced E/W runway and a 24-inch rotating beacon on an 800-acre site. Pan American Airways used the large hangar in the left center and a former yacht harbor to the left, not shown in the photograph, to launch their flying boats. (WTL.)

Alameda Airport had a new passenger terminal as well as hangars to support both airline traffic and private flying. Maddux Airlines Ford trimotors flew between Alameda and Los Angeles in 1929. The covered walkway was the 1920s version of today's airliner Jetway. (Larkins collection.)

In 1935, two famous men, Wiley Post and Will Rogers, were killed in the crash of Post's modified Lockheed *Orion* in Alaska. The bodies were brought to Seattle where they were then flown in a Pan American Airways (PAA) Douglas DC-2 to Los Angeles. This photograph shows the DC-2 landing at the PAA base at Alameda on August 19 for refueling. (Larkins collection.)

Pan American Airways used the older Sikorsky S-42 to lay out their routes in the Pacific before there were any passengers carried in the Martin 130. This view of their S-42B (NC-16734), the plane that was lost in an accident at Samoa with chief pilot Edwin Musick in November 1938, shows the large radio antennas that were built at their Alameda base for long-range Pacific communication. (WTL.)

The Martin M-130 "China Clipper" was the first of the Pan American flying boats to carry passengers and mail in the Pacific. Each of the four M-130s had a different name; however, because NC-14716—the "China Clipper"—received all of the vast publicity for the first mail flight from Alameda to Manila in November 1935, the name has become synonymous with Pan American Clippers. This 1936 photograph shows the primitive conditions at their Alameda base compared with today's extensive airports. (WTL.)

Eleven years before NAS Alameda opened there were navy planes on the island. This new Boeing F4B-1 is at Alameda Airport in July 1929 on its way from Seattle to NAS San Diego, where it was assigned to Fighter Squadron One (VF-1B) on the USS *Saratoga* (CV-3). (R. L. Dickson.)

Earlier, on May 10, 1929, these two Martin T4M-1s from Torpedo Squadron One (VT-1B), also assigned to the aircraft carrier USS *Lexington* (CV-2), are shown inside one of the large hangars at the east end of the Curtiss-Wright Field/Alameda Airport. (R. L. Dickson.)

In July 1938, Howard Hughes and a crew of four flew around the world in three days in this modified Lockheed 14, leaving from and returning to New York City. It is shown here at San Francisco Bay Airdrome in Alameda during a visit in the summer of 1940. (WTL.)

If Benton Field Air Depot in Alameda had been completed and the land had not been turned over to the navy instead it could have been a large Army Air Corps supply and transport base, with hangars and runways for planes such as this Douglas C-39 of the 62nd Transport Group, activated in December 1940 at the Sacramento Air Depot. (WTL.)

Two

Naval Air Station Alameda

This 1960s aerial photograph, taken from over the estuary, shows the Main Street gate. The center of the photo shows the display aircraft, parade ground and grass area leading to the Administration building. Cargo ships are at Piers 2 and 3 in the distance. Streets were named for carriers such as Lexington, Saratoga, Hancock, Midway, Ranger, and so on, as well as naval air stations such as Pearl Harbor, Barbers Point, Norfolk, Glenview, Pensacola, Corpus Christi, and Marine Corps Air Station El Toro. (USN.)

Capt. Frank R. McCrary, center, was brought out of retirement to become the first commanding officer of Naval Air Station Alameda in 1940. Comdr. John G. Farrell, on the left, was the first executive officer assisted by Comdr. Henry T. Stanley, on the right. (USN.)

A photograph taken during the commissioning ceremony shows, from left to right, Adm. Arthur Hepburn, 12th Naval District commandant; Capt. Frank McCrary; and army general John DeWitt. (USN.)

This 1940 aerial photograph shows the slow process of the landfill and the start of the Seaplane Lagoon, seen in the upper right corner. All the descriptions of the early construction of Naval Air Station Alameda describe the difficulties of working in the mud. (WTL.)

An interesting 1957 aerial photograph taken by the NAS Oakland Reserve shows their ZSG-2 airship (blimp) of VP-871 flying over the southern end of the air station. This area, and more not shown to the right, was used for years as a storage area for aircraft. A Convair R3Y-1 Tradewind minus its props sits in the lower right corner. (USN.)

The first official plane assigned to NAS Alameda was this Grumman J2F-4 (BuNo 1651) from Utility Squadron 6. This photograph taken at Oakland Airport in January 1941 shows the historic number "1" and station name on the side. A small Fairchild JK-1 (civilian Model 45) had been assigned to Captain McCrary in 1940 during the initial period of construction before the air station was commissioned. (WTL.)

This elderly 1930s Grumman SF-1 (BuNo 9487) became *Alameda-2* after service with the Oakland naval reserve. It was photographed outside Hangar 3 at Oakland Airport, the home of Naval Reserve Aviation Base Oakland. A new Grumman JRF-4 Goose became *Alameda-4* in 1941. In an unusual twist of fate, a civilian JRF-4 flew from Alameda 54 years later to qualify for transport to Hawaii on the USS *Carl Vinson* (CVN–70) as described on page 48. (Peter Bowers.)

This Lockheed 18 Lodestar was used as a navy R5O-3 command transport assigned to station operations in 1943. The photograph shows it in March 1946 with the rare flag rank markings of a one-star commodore. The star can be seen on the engine nacelle and the name *Alameda* near the door. (WTL.)

Rank hath its privileges, and this photograph of a North American SNJ-6 shows an example of a "common" advanced trainer converted to a highly polished station aircraft, with blue and gold trim on the anti-glare panel and prop spinner. This plane was photographed over Concord, California, in March 1947. (WTL.)

Another unusual aircraft at Alameda was this Beech SNB-2C modified as an SNB-2HP. The dual use as a hospital plane and photographic plane gave it the unusual model designation suffix of "HP." The photograph was taken at NAS Alameda in March 1946. (WTL.)

Scout Observation Service Unit Three (SOSU-3) was an active squadron at Alameda for transition training of pilots to be assigned to battleship and cruiser catapult aircraft. This Curtiss SOC-2, photographed in January 1946, was the personal plane of the commanding officer, painted in postwar dark blue with a yellow "W" for SOSU-3. (Peter Bowers.)

This Japanese Aichi M6A Seiran, a submarine-based attack plane, was part of a large display of navy aircraft for the 20th anniversary of the air station in September 1960. In addition, it has a rare Yokosuka MXY-7 Ohka rocket-powered piloted suicide plane called the "Baka Bomb" by the United States shown on the left and an experimental Douglas D-558-1 Skystreak on the right. Several Japanese types were among the aircraft exhibited to some 60,000 visitors at an "End of the War Open House" in August 1945. (USN.)

The Cessna T-50 five-passenger transport was widely used by the Army Air Force as well as the navy. This JRC-1 (Utility Transport Cessna Model One) served at NAS Alameda before being declared surplus and sold at San Jose by the War Assets Administration in 1945. (WTL.)

At the start of World War II there was a desperate need for long-range, four-engine transports so the navy assigned the one and only experimental Sikorsky XPBS-1 to fly VIP personnel and critical parts to the Pacific. There was a precedent to this when the secretary of the navy Frank Knox passed through the Bay Area in 1940 aboard the Consolidated XPB2Y-1. As NAS Alameda did not exist at the time, the plane moored overnight at the Pan American Airways lagoon at Treasure Island. (USN.)

On June 30, 1942, Adm. Chester Nimitz, commander in chief of the Pacific Fleet, and some of his staff members carrying important wartime planning papers arrived at the San Francisco Bay from Hawaii. Just as the XPBS-1 was touching down on the water it hit a submerged log, a common hazard in the bay, nosed down, and went on its back. Somehow all escaped except for the copilot, and Admiral Nimitz was able to go to the St. Francis Hotel in San Francisco that evening. (USN.)

This photograph, taken on May 5, 1947, shows over 400 Grumman F6F Hellcats awaiting overhaul or scrapping at the west end of the air station alongside the Oakland Estuary. The main runways can be seen in the background. Most were repaired, painted, and delivered to naval reserve bases throughout the country, including NAS Oakland. The massive production line for this operation can be seen in the photograph on page 51. (WTL.)

This smaller group shows Grumman F7F-3P Tigercats stored on the Marston mats in the "Bone yard" near Encinal High School, in the southeast corner of Alameda Naval Air Station, in July 1946. They are Marine Corps planes shipped back from the Pacific, probably from squadron VMP-254. (WTL.)

This aerial view taken from the north side of the Oakland Inner Harbor (estuary) shows the Moore Dry Dock Company in the foreground and Todd Shipyard beyond the ship on the left. The rows of buildings in the left center are 976 navy public quarters (enlisted families) off the base. The large buildings in the center, bordering on Main Street, are warehouses, and the area on the right with the trees had 51 single-family units for senior officers, including two for admirals. (WTL.)

A navy aerographer studies a weather report to be given to the control tower to broadcast to aircraft approaching NAS Alameda. Weather reporting was and is critical for flight safety. (USN.)

The most important activity for the airfield was the control tower. The aircraft controllers directed all aircraft movements on the ground as well as approving takeoff procedures and instructions for landing aircraft. It was staffed by officers and enlisted men 24 hours a day, and the ramp in front of it was used for visiting admirals and other special flights. The building has been saved temporarily as part of Alameda Point. (See chapter 7.) (USN.)

Navy control tower operators were not only navy trained but examined and certified by the Civil Aeronautics Administration (CAA, now FAA) on an equal basis with government civilian air traffic controllers. This 1950s photograph shows San Francisco and the Bay Bridge in the upper background. (USN.)

NAS Cinema, the station theater on Third Street, showed all major motion pictures in the evening and had a children's matinee on Saturday afternoons. Additional recreational facilities were a children's center, community center, party hut, picnic area, bowling lanes, craft hobby shop, gymnasium, golf course, swimming pool, yacht club, and an aero club. (USN.)

NAS Alameda had a complete U.S. Post Office on Third Street and Avenue B for the use of active duty military, dependent families, and civilian civil service workers. (USN.)

The well-known officers club on Main Street facing the estuary was the center of social activities day and night and fondly remembered by thousands of officers, their wives, and guests. One wall of the bar was covered with squadron insignias formally mounted on wooden plaques. The club has been saved from destruction and is currently being operated by a private concern as part of Alameda Point redevelopment. (WTL.)

In addition to the Commissioned Officer's Mess (club) and a Chief Petty Officer's Mess (club) for grades E-6 through E-9, there was a White Hat Club (Enlisted Men's Club) for sailors to use on off-duty hours. All three offered lunch, dinner, and cocktails. (USN.)

The Station Chapel at Avenue A and Third Street provided services for all faiths by the navy chaplains. Military personnel, their family members, friends, and relatives were all invited, and in addition to nursery care, baptisms and weddings were performed. (USN.)

The beautiful "Arch of Swords" is approved for officers who elect the formal dress and ceremony for a wedding or retirement. It is performed at the end of the wedding when the bride and groom leave the chapel and walk beneath the swords held by his fellow officers. In this photograph, Lt. James Perrizo, a pilot with Alameda Reserve Squadrons HS-872 and VS-38, and his bride, Helene Martin, exit the chapel in August 1964. (USN.)

In a scene that enlisted men of all services are familiar with, this photograph shows the waiting line for daily meals at the general mess in Building 3 on First Street. Food service for thousands of men is a monumental task on any large military base. (USN.)

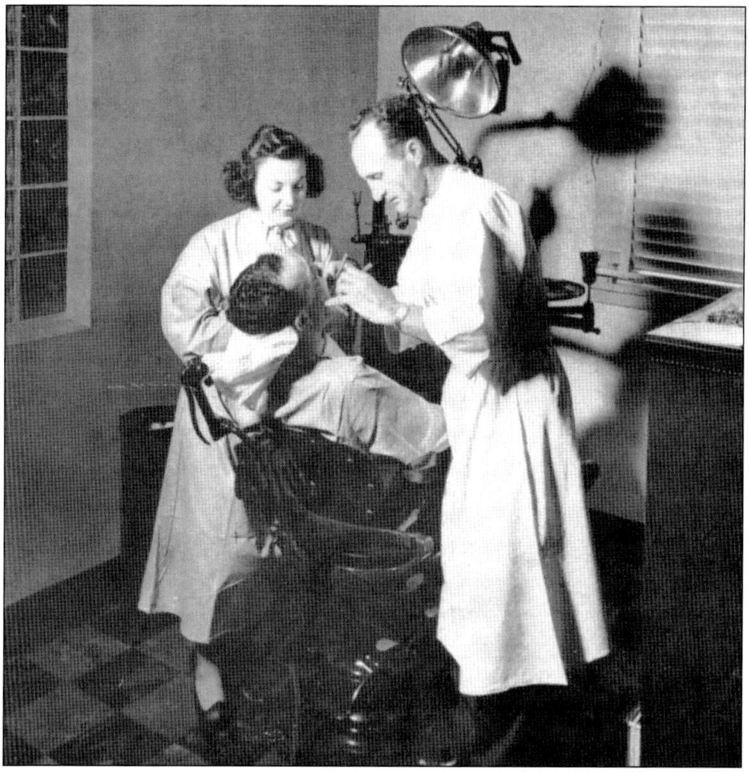

Every naval air station has medical and dental service. Medical and dental offices at NAS Alameda were in Building 16 at Third Street and Avenue B. This historic wartime photograph illustrates early dental work being done in 1942. (USN.)

This 1942 photograph shows a portion of the telephone switchboard operated 24 hours a day at the air station. The communications department was vital to the operation of the naval air station in wartime. (USN.)

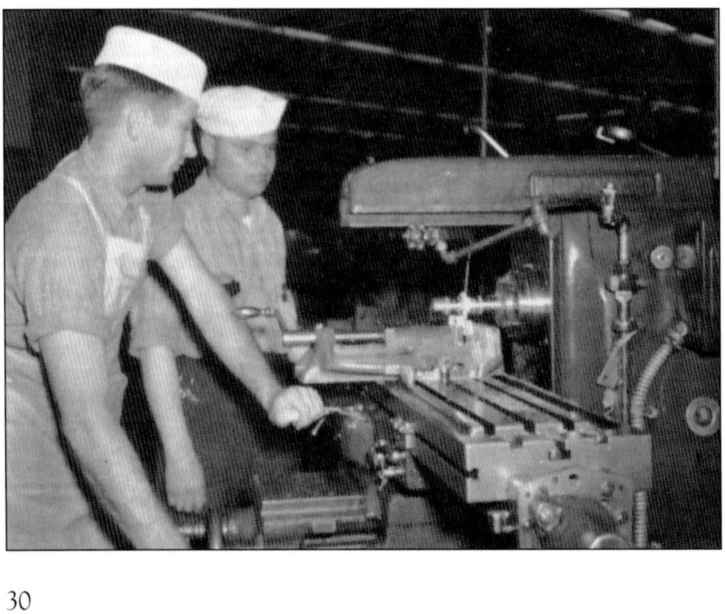

During the first year of World War II, before thousands of civilian workers were hired and trained, the work in the Assembly and Repair Department was done by active-duty, navy-enlisted men as shown in this photograph. This experience was crucial to the rapid expansion of naval aviation and the need for skilled mechanics aboard aircraft carriers and at overseas bases. (USN.)

Enlisted and officer WAVES (Women Accepted for Voluntary Emergency Service) served in many capacities in World War II. Their duties at NAS Alameda ranged from office work to control tower operators, and in both squadron support and overhaul and repair. WAVES were still serving at Alameda in 1962. (USN.)

In addition to providing security for the air station, the marine barracks personnel served as the color guard for daily and special occasions and the honor guard for visiting dignitaries but were perhaps best known for service at the main gate for 56 years. (USN.)

A flood at the main gate on January 9, 1970, provided a unique view of the entrance to the air station. This shows Building 30 and the main gate after a high tide of 7.3 feet and a 30-knot wind the previous midnight. (USN.)

A break in a water main under the street caused this common sight in the late 1940s. The air station is only 10 feet above sea level with much of it built on fill so a sinkhole is not unusual. (USN.)

This 1989 Pierce Arrow is Engine No. 3 at Station 1. It had a capacity of 500 gallons of water and 100 gallons of foam. The pumper was capable of putting out 1,000 gallons per minute. Engine No. 2 was at Station 2. (Dino Torres.)

Fire captain Dino Torres, on the right, is directing a training exercise involving a motor vehicle. NAS Alameda had its own fire department as indicated by the name on the helmets. (Dino Torres.)

All aircraft were loaded and off-loaded from the aircraft carriers at Alameda from 1941 to 1961, when NAS Lemoore was opened in the California Central Valley. After that, the planes flew off the carrier before it docked and returned when the ship was at sea after leaving Alameda. A few aircraft, such as this Grumman A-6, were still lifted aboard carriers at Alameda by the huge cranes after the change. (Douglas Olson.)

This photograph shows the procedure for loading a Douglas A-4 Skyhawk with one of the large cranes. These motorized cranes traveled on railroad tracks to and from the dock to load and unload planes from the aircraft carriers. (USN.)

This Grumman F6F-5 Hellcat was fresh out of overhaul when photographed in February 1947. The handwritten words "RUN IN" on the tail indicated that the engine was ready for flight after a thorough ground test. The name on the side is Ens. Ken Adams. (WTL.)

This Douglas AD-3 Skyraider had engine trouble while flying out of Alameda and had to make an emergency landing at Buchanan Field, the Contra Costa County Airport, in November 1951. A navy crew from Alameda with a new engine drove to the airport and changed engines "in the field" so that the plane could fly back to the air station. (WTL.)

Air Scout Hellcat Squadron 7 was one of the youth programs at NAS Alameda, and this special photograph shows their overnight camp at Lincoln Park in May 1947 with the Vought-Sikorsky OS2U-3 Kingfisher loaned to them by Scout Observation Service Squadron Three. (WTL.)

Boys are always fascinated by guns and the annual Armed Forces Day Open House celebrations offered a chance to see and touch the actual weapons. This photograph captures an entranced lad handling a machine gun on a Marine Corps Sikorsky UH-34J helicopter. (WTL.)

The 1968 Desilu motion picture *Yours, Mine and Ours* did much of its filming at NAS Alameda. In this scene Henry Fonda is loading up groceries in the commissary for his wife, played by Lucille Ball, and the 20 children from their combined marriage. Van Johnson also starred in the film that was a comedy based on the true story of the Beardsley family. (USN.)

Hollywood actor Robert Stack, who once worked for NARF, poses with a group of employees during a visit to the Alameda Naval Aviation Depot (NADEP) facility. (USN.)

This insignia or logo for Naval Air Station Alameda was used for station publications and signs as well as a cloth patch that has become a collectable item. The naval aviator wings cover the world. NAS Alameda is in the upper right, and a jet fighter is headed northwest over the San Francisco-Oakland Bay Bridge. (USN.)

This was the mold for a new large Naval Air Rework Facility (NARF) insignia to be mounted on the outside wall of Building 5A. It was constructed under the supervision of Robert Jessen, head of the Pattern Shop, with Sally Lomax, fiberglass specialist, and Al Beasley, a joiner, working together on the project with the help of six apprentices. (USN.)

This civilian Curtiss C-46 cargo plane is an example of a lesser-known service to the navy. QUICKTRANS was an acronym for expedited commercial airlift of navy supplies by civilian contract. BUSANDA was the Bureau of Supplies and Accounts that was disestablished in 1966, shortly after this photograph was taken in 1965. (WTL.)

Long since torn down, the three tall checkered water towers were a landmark on the air station. One was 151 feet high and held 200,000 gallons of water. In this view of a Douglas A-4B from VA-164, taken in July 1963, one of the towers can be seen on the extreme right. (WTL.)

This Piper UO-1, used as a small air station short-range transport, was a military procurement of the civilian six-passenger Piper *Aztec*. This photograph of Alameda's UO-1 was in April 1961, before the U.S. Department of Defense reorganization of aircraft designations changed it to U-11A in September 1962. See page 21 for Alameda's wartime equivalent. (WTL.)

In December 1964, a Presidential Unit Citation, signed by secretary of the navy Paul Nitze and Pres. Lyndon Johnston, was awarded to NAS Alameda. It read, "In special recognition of an outstanding contribution to greater economy and improvement in Government operations during the tenth anniversary year of the Federal incentive awards program." (USN.)

Vice Pres. Hubert Humphrey arrives at NAS Alameda in the 1960s aboard this Lockheed VC-140B JetStar of the presidential fleet based at Andrews Air Force Base. Six of these small VIP transports were operated by the U.S. Air Force. (USN.)

Vice Pres. Hubert Humphrey spoke to an assembled group upon his arrival at Naval Air Station Alameda from this podium set up on the flight line next to his plane. Vice Pres. Dan Quayle flew into the air station in 1989 to view the earthquake damage in the area. (USN.)

Pres. John F. Kennedy flew into NAS Alameda in Air Force One in March 1962 in order to give an address at the University of California, Berkeley. This photograph shows him about to get into the presidential limousine at the head of the motorcade. The honor guard on the right consisted of U.S. Navy, Marine Corps, and Air Force enlisted men. A small portion of the hundreds of station employees that lined the route can be seen at the top left of the photograph. (USN.)

In August 1993, Pres. William Clinton spoke in front of the USS *Carl Vinson* (CVN-70) at Alameda describing his five-point plan for base closure and authorized an expenditure of $25 million for an environmental technology demonstration fund to pilot a University of California, Berkeley/ Lawrence Livermore Laboratory environmental cleanup program at NAS Alameda. (USN.)

The airfield portion of NAS Alameda was formally dedicated as Nimitz Field in 1967 during a large ceremony in Hangar 11. As part of this dedication a bronze plaque was designed by William Huff, a skilled artist and employee of the O&R Pattern Shop. This photograph shows Huff and Catherine Nimitz, wife of Chester Nimitz, examining the memorial, which reads, "NIMITZ FIELD / In commemoration of Fleet Admiral Chester William Nimitz, United States Navy (February 24, 1885–February 20, 1966). His excellence in command leadership was a primary source of victory in war—and strength in peace. This field is dedicated to his memory. January 26, 1967." (USN.)

Catherine Nimitz presses the button that activated a mechanism that unveiled the memorial plaque designating the airfield at NAS Alameda as "Nimitz Field" in honor of her late husband, Fleet Admiral Chester Nimitz. Capt. Duncan A. Campbell, commanding officer of NAS Alameda, stands behind her to the left. (USN.)

Although this photograph was taken in 2004 after the air station was closed, it shows the size and complexity of NAS Alameda and a 1952 mission statement describes it in more detail: "Provide facilities to support regular operations of fleet carrier reconnaissance, anti-submarine, and transport aircraft. Support the Aircraft Overhaul and Repair Program and serve as primary aviation supply point including an aeronautical outfitting assembly point. Fleet and other major activities will include Headquarters for Commander Fleet Air Alameda, Fleet Logistic Wing Pacific, Naval Air Bases Twelfth Naval District and Alameda Group of the Pacific Reserve Fleet. One Carrier Air Group and seven squadrons, plus a Fleet airborne electronics training unit detachment were listed at that time." (WTL.)

This early aerial photograph shows five of the facilities used by the Assembly and Repair Department in 1948. No. 1 is Hangar 23, No. 2 is the Bombsight Building, No. 3 is the Interim Overhaul Building, No. 4 is the main Assembly and Repair Building, and No. 5 shows the north end of Hangar 11. The control tower is in the lower right corner surrounded by interesting World War II planes. (USN.)

This second aerial photograph shows No. 1, the Salvage Building; No. 2, the Engine Overhaul Building; and No. 3, the Engine Test Stand facility. The northeast corner of the Seaplane Lagoon can be seen in the lower left with Consolidated PBY Catalinas lined up on the ramp. (USN.)

A small practice landing field was built as an auxiliary to NAS Alameda with the lesser-known name of OLF Concord. The definition was "Outlying Field," and planes were sent there for practice landings to ease the air traffic at Alameda. This photograph shows a Douglas SBD-5 Dauntless landing there in March 1944. Additional naval auxiliary airfields were established at Crows Landing, Cotati, Hollister, Santa Rosa, and Vernalis. (WTL.)

This photograph of a Vought-Sikorsky OS2U-2 Kingfisher taking off from OLF Concord in March 1944 shows the open country surrounding the field and the absence of buildings. Other types known to use the field were the Beech SNB-1 and 2C, Cessna JRC-1, Grumman F4F-3, F6F-5, and TBM-3. (WTL.)

North American B-25J *In The Mood* jumps into the air at full power on August 11, 1995, to be evaluated and approved for carrier takeoff from the USS *Carl Vinson* (CVN-70) when it arrives in Honolulu to take part in a massive VJ Day celebration. The runway was marked at 100, 200, and 300 feet from the start, with 50-foot marks thereafter. Navy men and others were stationed at these spots to verify the takeoff distance for each plane being tested, and the limit was 800 feet. (WTL.)

The Grumman FM-2 taxis out past Hangar 20, where the warbirds were kept, on its way to its takeoff test on Runway 25. Three B-25s, as well as an FG-1D, F4U-5N, FM-2, TBM-3E, SNJ-5, JRF-4, and HU-16C, went to Hawaii on the USS *Carl Vinson* in 1995 to participate in the World War II VJ Day celebration there. All of the aircraft took off from the carrier deck to take part in a massive flyby of over 100 planes for President Clinton and thousands of viewers. (WTL.)

This view of a Consolidated PBY-5A Catalina parked next to the tower with the San Francisco skyline in the background in 1990 is a fitting reminder that Patrol Squadron Forty Four (VP-44) began arriving at NAS Alameda from Seattle on January 3, 1941, with PBY-5 flying boats. The squadron was re-designated as VP-61 on January 6 to form Patrol Wing 61. (WTL.)

This North American SNJ-5 Texan was one of several civilian-restored military aircraft, now known as "Warbirds," that attended the 50th anniversary open house at NAS Alameda on October 3, 1990. It included two rare, privately owned Douglas AD Skyraiders, a former AAF Vultee BT-13A painted as a navy SNV-1 trainer, as well as other types. (WTL.)

This Douglas A-4C Skyhawk greeted U.S. Navy personnel and visitors alike as they entered the main gate at the end of Main Street on the north end of the air station. It was between the gate and the administration building. Unfortunately, after the air station closed, a violent windstorm tilted it off the pedestal, and it had to be removed. It is now being restored. (See chapter 7.) (WTL.)

Another well-cared-for exhibit aircraft was mounted on a pylon on a landscaped traffic island inside the east gate on Atlantic Avenue. This Ling-Temco-Vought A-7A Corsair II has been well cared for even after the base closure. A photograph of it in 2009 is in chapter 7. (WTL.)

Three

A&R, O&R, NARF, AND NADEP

This interior photograph of the Overhaul and Repair Department shows a production line equal to that found in the aircraft industry. The impressive lineup of Grumman F6F Hellcats illustrates the overhaul of the F6Fs shown on page 23. The repair facility at Alameda started as the Assembly and Repair Department in 1941, changed to Overhaul and Repair Department in 1948, to Naval Air Rework Facility in 1967 under the Naval Air Systems Command, and finally to Naval Air Depot in 1987. It remained under that name until its closure in 1997 by the Base Realignment and Closure Act of 1990. The skilled civilian workforce that reached 9,500 in 1945 had been reduced to 3,500 by 1991, and the overhaul of aircraft and engines was replaced in part by an emphasis on sophisticated electronics, guided missiles, and even the repair of a generator engine for Spruance-class destroyers. (USN.)

The first overhaul program of the new Assembly and Repair Department was for the Curtiss SOC Seagull. This two-place biplane operated on a single float from a catapult on almost all of the cruisers and battleships in the fleet. This photograph shows the 16th plane (SOC-2 Serial No. 0423) arriving in June 1941 from the cruiser *Minneapolis* (CA-36). The first plane was SOC-1 No. 9937, arriving February 3 and leaving overhaul on May 12, 1941. (WTL.)

This photograph is purported to be of No. 9937, the first plane completed by the Assembly and Repair Department. It clearly shows the majority of the workers as active-duty, navy-enlisted men. This changed quickly as World War II progressed, and from then on to the closure of the air station the work was done primarily by civilian civil service workers. (USN.)

Parachute inspection and repair, as well as life rafts and other life-saving devices, were part of the services supplied by the Assembly and Repair Department. (USN.)

The Propeller Shop is shown in Building 167 when it was part of Assembly and Repair in 1945. (USN.)

Robina McGregor Masterson is cleaning instrument dials in the Overhaul and Repair Instrument Shop in June 1948. Protection against radium exposure was strict at that time but not as severe as in later years. For more information, see chapter 7. (USN.)

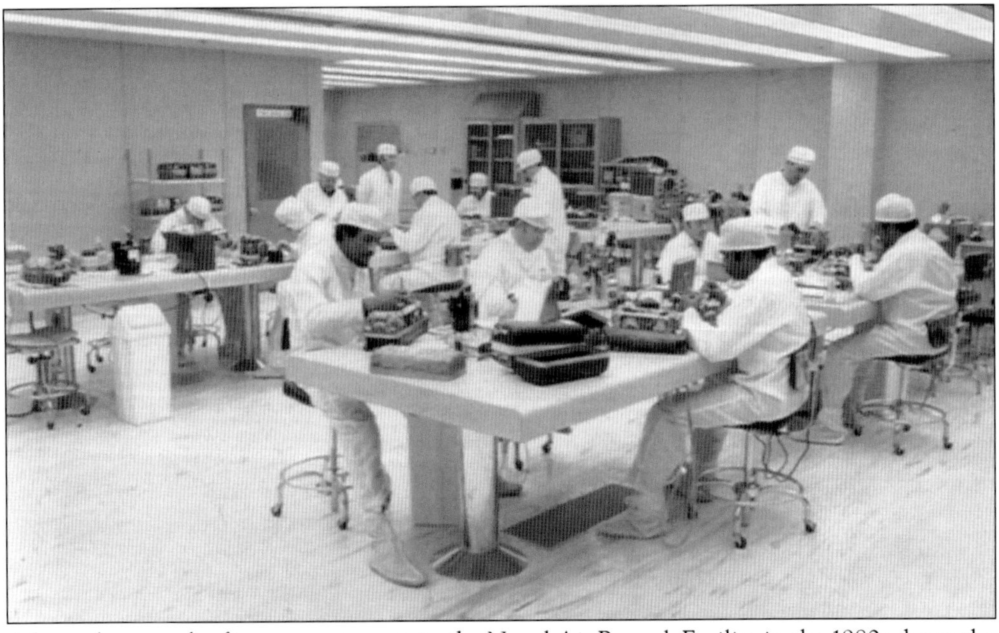

A later photograph of instrument repair in the Naval Air Rework Facility in the 1980s shows the increased protection with "Moon Suits" and other changes. (USN.)

An interior view is shown of the Radio and Radar Laboratory inspection and testing area in the Assembly and Repair Department in 1945. (USN.)

This photograph shows a similar view of the radio and radar machine shop in the Assembly and Repair Department in September 1945. (USN.)

The Overhaul and Repair Department managed these remarkable automated engine parts stacks. (USN.)

This is about one-half of the fuselage, plus the wing stubs, of a Douglas A-4 Skyhawk on the overhead moving crane used to save floor space by transporting large units from one section of assembly to another. (USN.)

New, larger exhaust stacks were installed on the Engine Test Cells building with acoustical properties to reduce the noise level from jet engine tests. The Aircraft Acoustical Enclosure was added in 1991. (USN.)

This is an interior view of one of the Engine Test Cells with a turboprop jet engine being prepared for a test run. (USN.)

Capt. R. S. Miller, commanding officer of NARF; and Bryce Mirko, board chairman, stand in front of the A-7 pilot rework board members with the first Ling-Temco-Vought Corsair II to be inducted into the Progressive Aircraft Rework Program at NARF. (USN.)

In April 1995, Alameda delivered the last of 23 Grumman A-6s that were re-winged by the station naval aviation depot. (USN.)

Comdr. J. O. Coleman, executive officer of Patrol Squadron One (VP-1) at NAS Whidbey Island, accepts the last Lockheed P2V-7 Neptune overhauled at Alameda from Capt. Rupert S. Miller, commanding officer of Naval Rework Facility Alameda. In the background are, from left to right, Deno Lenzi; James Harris; Paul Armknecht; Basil Antoneko; John Taylor; Comdr. C. E. Boeing, executive officer of NARF; Stephen Duncan; Lt. L. J. LeDoux; Francis Casella; Lt. D. R. Johnson; ADJ James Smith; Frank West; Willard Smith; Gladys Williams; and Robert Williams. (USN.)

The navy's rework facilities bid against each other for the contract to overhaul all of the same type of aircraft for the fleet. NARF Alameda was given the Douglas A-4 Skyhawk assignment as can be seen in this photograph of the lineup of A-4s. (USN.)

Striping, cleaning, and repainting was a major operation at Alameda. One of the more unusual jobs was this Lockheed US-3A, the S-3A Viking antisubmarine plane modified as a six-passenger Carrier-Onboard-Delivery transport. The O&R Epoxy Paint Shop eventually grew to become the new, large building shown in chapter 7. (USN.)

A flight test crew is about to make an acceptance flight of a Lockheed P-3A Orion after its complete overhaul by the NARF. In 1991, NADEP started a program to modify Lockheed P-3Cs to the EP-3E Aires II. Each aircraft required 50,000 man-hours of work and 33,000 parts in the modification kit. (USN.)

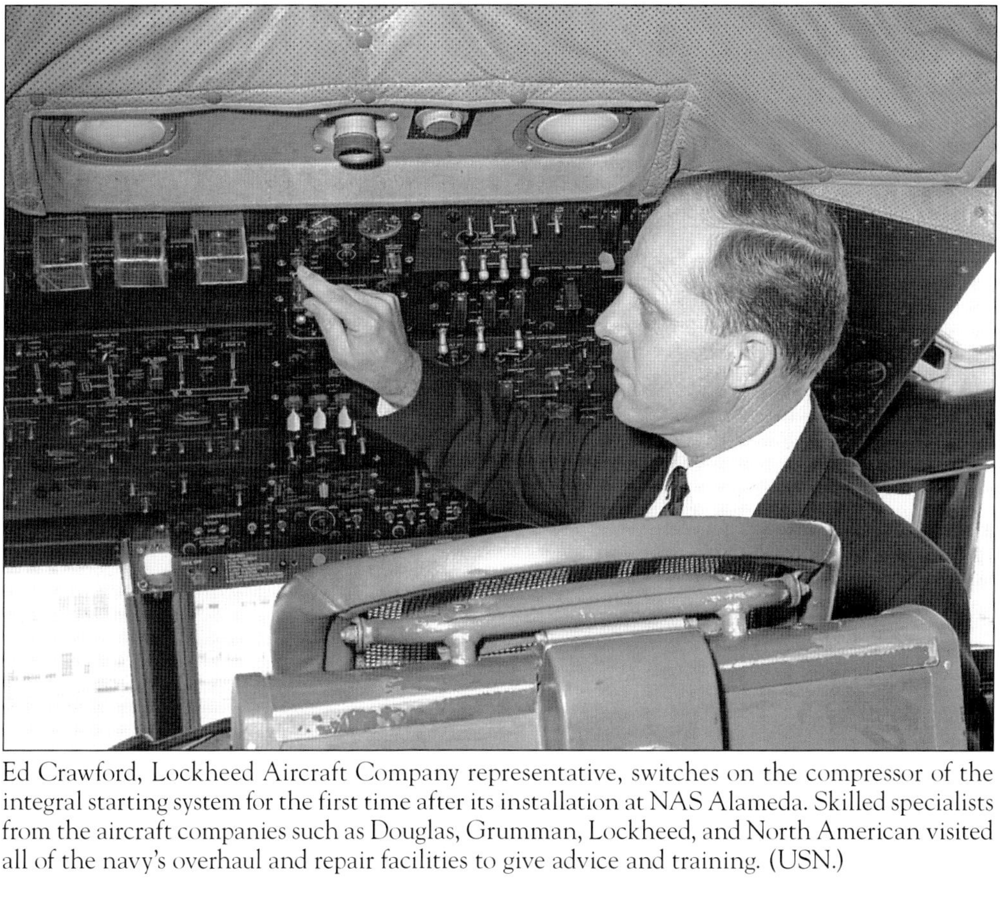

Ed Crawford, Lockheed Aircraft Company representative, switches on the compressor of the integral starting system for the first time after its installation at NAS Alameda. Skilled specialists from the aircraft companies such as Douglas, Grumman, Lockheed, and North American visited all of the navy's overhaul and repair facilities to give advice and training. (USN.)

The escort carrier *Cape Esperance* (CVE-88) is shown entering San Francisco Bay in August 1958 while being used by the Military Sea Transportation Service to transport aircraft and parts from the Pacific area to NAS Alameda. The deck load shown is four North American FJ Furys and two Grumman F6F Hellcats. (WTL.)

This North American FJ-3D Fury shows the preparation for protection against salt air while being transported on the open deck of an escort carrier. All openings are sealed against excess moisture as well as the cockpit canopy. (WTL.)

This photograph of a North American FJ-3 (BuNo 136025) shows the extensive inspection involved in overhauling and returning a squadron plane to active duty. Every inspection panel and removable section has to be opened, cleaned, examined, and reconditioned by the Naval Air Rework Facility. (Deward Gresham.)

Lt. Comdr. Terry Howell retired as head of the flight check department of the Naval Air Rework Facility in 1980. He was "piped over the side" by his fellow officers in the formal ceremony similar to that approved for weddings (see page 28.). Every plane overhauled at NARF was flight tested before delivery to the fleet. (USN.)

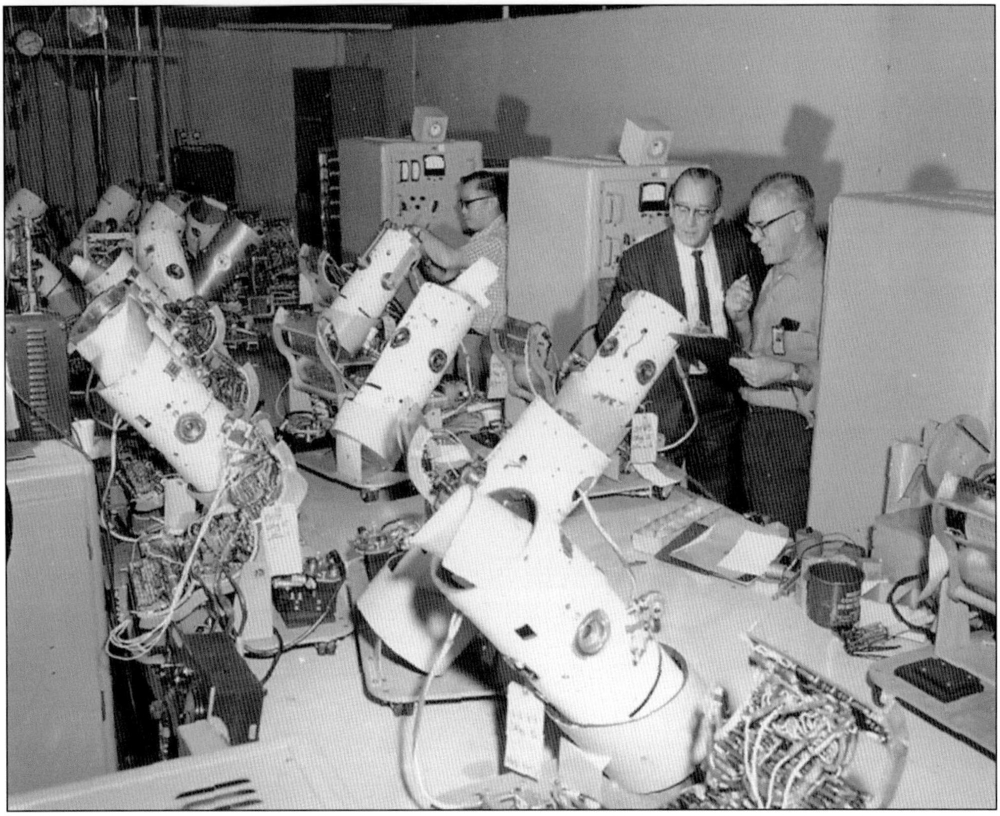

Detailed work on the missile guidance systems was performed by O&R, NARF, and NADEP over the years. NARF inspected, repaired, or modified some 3,000 Phoenix, Shrike, and Sparrow guided missiles in one year. (USN.)

Electronic engineers and technicians of the A3/Missile Engineering Division Branch are shown here posed outside of their building in the 1990s. (USN.)

This photograph shows the Assembly and Repair Building office in September 1945. (USN.)

The Toastmaster Club was one of several groups for civilian employees. From left to right are Richard L. Smith with his "Clam Shell" award for not talking long enough, Everitt O. Knott with the "Lady" award for giving the best speech, and Boyd Woodmansee with his "Windbag" award for talking too long. All three men were from the Overhaul and Repair Quality Assurance Group.

A large group of civilian employees are shown with "Zero Defects Group Performance Awards." Employees of NARF submitted 2,458 beneficial suggestions during a five-year period, starting in 1967, in which 1.607 aircraft, 9,356 engines, 25,573 missiles, and 511,813 components were overhauled. The later NADEP had 3,500 employees working on the Grumman A-6 Intruder, Grumman EA-6B Prowler, and the Lockheed S-3 Viking. (USN.)

Three employees with NARF Zero Defects Awards are, from left to right, Walter Blackwell Jr., Irene Gantt, and Melba Coveney. Terence Masterson is standing on the left side of the photograph. In 1970, NARF had 8,000 employees in 55 buildings. (USN.)

NAS Alameda had the first apprentice training program for naval aviation in 1946. The four-year program combined academic and shop training with the cooperation of the Alameda Unified School District. All of the men in the first class were veterans, so the GI Bill was also involved. Terence Masterson was in this first class. (USN.)

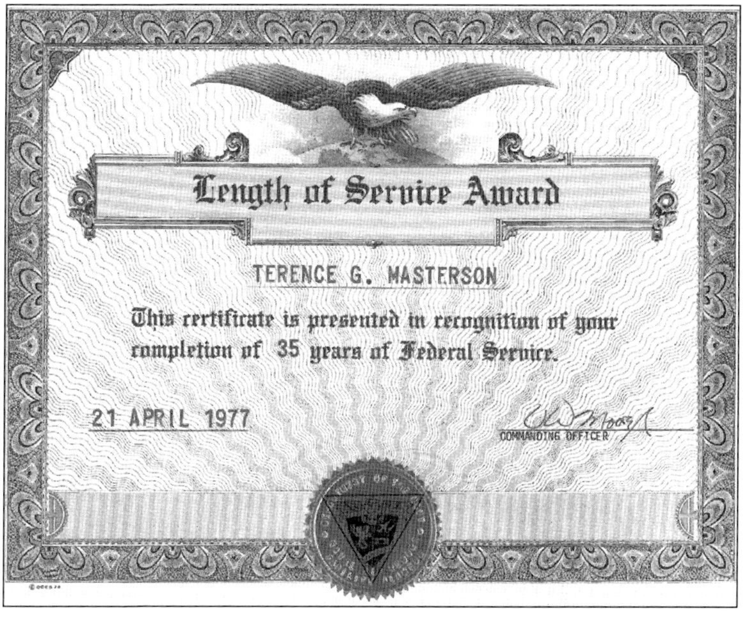

Length of Service Award

TERENCE G. MASTERSON

This certificate is presented in recognition of your completion of 35 years of Federal Service.

21 APRIL 1977

COMMANDING OFFICER

The high quality of the overhaul and repair facilities at O&R and NARF was partly the result of a large number of long-term skilled civil service employees. This certificate for 35 years of service at NAS Alameda is an example of how training and experience resulted in one employee going from apprentice to supervisor. (Robina Masterson.)

In 1957, approximately 50 Grumman S2F-1 antisubmarine planes were overhauled and cocooned for shipment to Japan as part of the Mutual Defense Treaty for the Japan Maritime Self-Defense Force. This photograph shows USN 136595 at Alameda in June 1957. (WTL.)

A similar program had been undertaken in 1965 to overhaul Navy Douglas A-1 Skyraiders for use by the U.S. Air Force in the Vietnam War. This photograph, taken on October 30, 1965, shows Navy 133095 just out of the Paint Shop the day before, with a cocooned 133867 in the right background. (WTL.)

Four

Squadron Activity

Except for the seaplanes, most of the squadron activity at NAS Alameda was by planes from aircraft carriers while they were in port. This photograph shows a Douglas AD-1 Skyraider from Attack Squadron Twenty (VA-20A) and a Grumman F8F-1 Bearcat from Fighter Squadron Twenty (VF-20A) from the BOXER CV-21. They are photographed over the Golden Gate Bridge by the author flying in the top turret of a Grumman TBM-3E Avenger flying out of Alameda Naval Air Station in June 1947. At least 72 squadrons and three carrier air groups were commissioned or decommissioned at NAS Alameda between 1941 and 1948. This included such little-known types as Evacuation Squadron (VE-3), Escort Scouting Squadron (VGS-33), Rescue Squadron (VH-3), and Night Torpedo Squadron (VTN-63). (WTL.)

The Martin PBM-3 and PBM-5 Mariner patrol bombers flew with Patrol Bombing Squadrons Sixteen (VPB-16) and One Four Five (VPB-145) based at NAS Alameda in 1944. Several were also modified into passenger transports and operated by VR-2 at Alameda, and 10 were flown by Pan American Airways, Pacific Division, at Treasure Island in 1943. (USN.)

The big four-engine Consolidated PB2Y-5 Coronado patrol bomber was also modified as a transport under the designation PB2Y-5R. Transport Squadron Two (VR-2) at Alameda had 44 of these assigned in December 1944 to carry passengers and cargo to and from Hawaii. (USN.)

The Martin JRM-2 Mars of Transport Squadron Two (VR-2) at Alameda established a remarkable record of carrying men and cargo to the Pacific. In 1949, the *Caroline Mars* carried 202 men from Alameda to San Diego. The last Mars flight ended at Alameda in August 1956. Each plane had an individual name, and this photograph shows the *Marianas Mars* headed out into the San Francisco Bay during high-speed taxi tests, escorted by Alameda's Piasecki HUP-3 helicopter. (USN.)

The Martin JRM-2 *Philippine Mars* demonstrates the size of the flying boat by having 95 sailors stand on the top of the 200-foot wing while it is at the loading dock at NAS Alameda in May 1949. The *Marshall Mars* carried a record 301 sailors from Air Group Five to San Diego in the same month. The prototype twin-tailed XPB2M-1R flew 78 trips between Alameda and Hawaii in World War II. (USN.)

The massive Lockheed XR6O-1 Constitution was the largest land transport ever flown from Alameda and the largest transport in the world at the time. The first of two was commissioned in a ceremony at NAS Alameda on February 2, 1949. It made a sensational short-field takeoff with the use of six JATO (Jet Assisted Take Off) bottles in order to clear the bridge. The following day it set a transcontinental record by flying from NAS Moffett Field to Washington, D.C., carrying 78 passengers and 18 crewmen for a record flight of 9 hours and 35 minutes. Its 189-foot span almost equaled that of the *Martin Mars*. The photograph shows it flying south past one of the towers of the San Francisco-Oakland Bay Bridge with the San Francisco waterfront in the background. (USN.)

The Douglas SBD Dauntless was the main dive bomber of World War II. This photograph shows two in flight in the Pacific in early 1944. Bombing Squadron Eighteen (VB-18) and Composite Squadron Thirty Seven (VC-37) with SBDs were commissioned at NAS Alameda in July 1943. (USN.)

The Curtiss SB2C-4 Helldiver was designed to replace the SBD, but both were used in the latter part of the war. This photograph shows one from Bombing Squadron Eight (VB-8) in 1943. Additional squadrons that were stationed at Alameda during the 1940s were VB-1, VB-17, VB-19, VB-82, and VB-153. Carrier Air Service Unit 6 had 76 Hellcats, 22 Helldivers, and 18 Avengers at Alameda in December 1944. (USN.)

The Grumman F9F-6 of Fighter Squadron One Five Three (VF-153) in the foreground is from one of the jet squadrons based at Alameda in the 1950s. No. 401, above, is from VF-154 based at NAS Moffett Field. They are over Korea in 1953 as part of the United Nations Police Action. This later became known as the Korean War. (USN.)

This Grumman F9F-8 Cougar from Fighter Squadron Ninety Three (VF-93) is an example of the planes that were stationed at Alameda in the 1950s and 1960s. Other squadrons during that period were VF-23, VF-52, VF-63, VF-64, VF-91, VF-92, VF-93, VF-94, VF-111, VF-151, VF-153, VF-192, VF-193, and VF-194. (WTL.)

This specially painted Grumman F8F-1, flying over San Francisco Ocean Beach in June 1947, was flown by LCDR D. C. "Whiff" Caldwell, commanding officer of Fighter Squadron Twenty (VF-20A) from the USS *Boxer* (CV-21). The painting of the pilot's ribbons on the cowling is very rare. (WTL.)

The sleek Grumman F11F-1 Tiger from Fighter Squadron One Nine One (VF-191) was another type of aircraft that was stationed at Alameda in the 1950s and 1960s. This photograph was taken in September 1959. Additional fighting squadrons at Alameda during that time were VF-21, VF-24, VFS-1, VFS-3, and Marine Corps Squadrons VMF-131 and VMF-141. (WTL.)

One of Scout Observation Service Unit Three's (SOSU-3) Curtiss SC-1 Seahawks is walked slowly down the ramp into the Seaplane Lagoon in 1946 for advanced transition flight training in order to fly from battleship and cruiser catapults with the fleet. Inshore patrol squadrons VS-47, VS-48, and VS-67 flew the Vought OS2U Kingfisher from Alameda in 1943. (Fred Dickey.)

This North American AJ-2 Savage of Heavy Attack Squadron Sixteen is an example of older aircraft that were put into the storage area at Alameda. VAH-16 was disestablished in January 1959 after operating for a year at NAS North Island. This photograph was taken in August 1960. (WTL.)

This photograph of a Martin P5M-2 Marlin of Patrol Squadron Forty Seven (VP-47) was taken on August 20, 1960, just four days before the squadron was scheduled to leave NAS Alameda. This was the last of the flying boats to be stationed at Alameda, ending a 29-year service started with the Consolidated PBY-4 Catalina in 1941. (Lawrence Smalley.)

The turboprop Convair R3Y-1 Tradewind was designed to be a 180,000-pound, high performance seaplane to replace the *Martin Mars*. Four were delivered to VR-2 at Alameda, but unfortunately problems persisted with the gearbox and contra rotating propellers, and in addition to other accidents VR-2s "Indian Ocean Tradewind" ran into the seawall at NAS Alameda with a runaway engine in January 1958. This photograph shows the "Caribbean Sea Tradewind" leaving Alameda in October 1956. (Peter Bowers.)

This Lockheed P2V-7 Neptune of Patrol Squadron Nine (VP-9) was photographed at Alameda in August 1960. VP-9 was stationed at NAS Alameda in the 1950s and 1960s as well as VP-47 and Reserve Squadron VP-871. (WTL.)

Patrol Squadron Nineteen (VP-19) was also stationed at Alameda with Lockheed Neptune P2V-7s in the 1950s and 1960s together with VP-4, VP-9, VP-28, VP-46, VP-47, VP-71, and 10 reserve patrol squadrons. (WTL.)

This beautiful formation flight of Douglas A-4 Skyhawks from Attack Squadron Ninety Four (VA-94) is representative of the attack squadrons based at Alameda in the 1960s. The others were VA-22, VA-23, VA-25, VA-52, VA-95, VA-112, VA-145, VA-152, VA-165, VA-215, VA-215, and VA-216. (USN.)

Capt. Daniel Weisenfeld, assistant O&R officer, and his crew pose after a successful acceptance flight test in March 1961 of a Douglas A3D-2P from the Overhaul and Repair Department. The flight suits and gear present an interesting contrast with the standard dress shown in the photograph below. (USN.)

Ens. Willard McWilliams demonstrates the more glamorous flight gear of the World War II period. He was assigned to Scout Observation Service Unit Three in 1945 for flight instruction in the Curtiss SC-1 Seahawk before being assigned to a battleship. The plane shown is one of several Vought-Sikorksy OS2U Kingfishers that were flown together with the SC-1s by SOSU-3 at this time. (Thomas McWillliams.)

Five Douglas A-1H Skyraiders are shown lined up outside the hangar in April 1964. Attack Squadron 215 (VA-215, the "Barn Owls") was based aboard the USS *Hancock* (CVA-19), homeported at Alameda Naval Air Station, and operating in the western Pacific. Five squadrons with A-1s were based at Alameda in the 1970s. (WTL.)

This Douglas AD-5Q of Carrier Airborne Early Warning Squadron Thirteen (VAW-13, the "Zappers") is shown outside of Hangar 22 on First Street in July 1962. Detachments from this Alameda-based squadron served aboard aircraft carriers with both the Pacific and Atlantic Fleets. The aircraft designation was changed to EA-1F in September 1962. (WTL.)

Transport Squadron Thirty (VR-30) flew the Convair C-131F Convair-Liner for several years as part of its "Navy Airline" fleet. It was a slightly modified military version of the Convair 340 used by airlines all over the United States. The VR-30 insignia can be seen on the nose in this photograph taken in May 1974 opposite Building 77. (WTL.)

Another military version of a standard airliner, the Douglas DC-9-30, was this C-9B Skytrain II flown by VR-30 to deliver passengers to and from NAS Alameda to air stations all over the United States. In 1975, a "Reserve Airlift" operated to bring Salt Lake City reservists to Alameda for their drill weekends. The U.S. Navy C-9B had a cargo door and could carry 100 passengers, and this one was photographed at Alameda in May 1974. (WTL.)

The smaller North American CT-39E Sabreliner was operated by Transport Squadron Thirty (VR-30) for shorter-range flights that only required seating for up to six passengers. It is shown here in front of the hangar in December 1974. (WTL.)

Clean and bright after being washed down near the Seaplane Lagoon, this Grumman C-1A Trader was photographed in October 1965. The C-1A was a modification of the S2F antisubmarine plane and carried passengers and cargo from land-based air stations to aircraft carriers at sea. (WTL.)

The author is shown here just after landing on the USS *Coral Sea* in the Grumman C-1A of Squadron VR-30 COD. The flight to the carrier off Monterey and back to NAS Alameda was on June 18, 1968. The Carrier-Onboard-Delivery flights were standard for the delivery of mail and passengers between land bases and aircraft carriers at sea. (USN.)

Five

Aircraft Carriers

This photograph shows the attack carrier USS *Coral Sea* (CVA-43) leaving for the western Pacific on July 26, 1967, with its full aircraft complement and crew aboard. Upon returning to Alameda from a 1968–1969 cruise in the western Pacific, the attack carrier *Coral Sea* (CVA-43) received its fourth Navy Unit Commendation Award, and its Air Wing 15 (CVW-15) gained its third award. Together they participated in 110 combat days and flew 1,531 sorties. The carrier held many open house days for visitors during the years that it was homeported at Alameda. (See page 96.) At least 30 aircraft carriers have been identified as being at NAS Alameda. One of the last aircraft carrier arrivals at Alameda was the USS *Abraham Lincoln* (CVN-72), returning from six months duty off the coast of Somalia in November 1993. (WTL.)

After World War II, one of the first aircraft carriers to arrive at Alameda was the USS *Boxer* (CV-21). This September 1947 photograph shows it in the bay where it was accompanied by the USS *Tarawa* (CV-40), USS *Valley Forge* (CV-45), and escort carrier *Bairoko* (CVE-115). (WTL.)

The *Bon Homme Richard* (CVA-31) is shown leaving Alameda on November 1, 1958, with the rare deck view of Grumman F11F-1s of VF-191 "Satan's Kittens." The other squadrons were VF-193 (with F3H-2s), VA-192 (FJ-4Bs), VA-195 (AD-6s), and VAH-2 (A3D-2s). (WTL.)

Few people other than navy men and some of their families have seen this view of the *Enterprise* island from above. Its distinctive design and shape made this atomic-powered aircraft carrier unique. The sailors are headed for San Francisco on June 21, 1966. (WTL.)

Attack Squadron Ninety Three (VA-93), the "Blue Blazers," comprised of Douglas A-4C Skyhawks, are shown here on the forward deck of the *Enterprise* as it returns from the western Pacific and Vietnam in June 1966. They exhibited a little squadron humor with the banner reading BLUE BOOZERS. Their name was changed to "The Fighting Ravens" in 1976. (WTL.)

One of the oldest carriers to operate from Alameda was the *Hancock* (CVA-19). It was commissioned in April 1944 with its angled deck completed in November 1956. This August 1959 photograph shows it leaving for its fourth WesPac Cruise with VF-151, VA-152, VA-153, VA-155, VCP-63, VAH-4, and VAW-11 aboard. (WTL.)

Hancock (CVA-19) is shown departing San Francisco in August 1969 with Air Wing 21 aboard, consisting of VF-211 "Checkmates," VF-24 "Checkertails," VA-212 "Rampant Raiders," VA-164 "Ghost Riders," VA-55 "Warhorses," VFP-63 Detachment 19 "Eyes of the Fleet," and VAW-111 Detachment 19 "Hunters." (WTL.)

The *Midway* (CVA-41), a 1945 ship, got an angled deck in 1957 just before this August 16, 1958, photograph. It shows F3H-2s of VF-64, A3D-2s of VAH-8 on the left and right, and FJ-4Bs of VA-63 down the middle. AD-6s of VA-65 are at the top of the photograph. (WTL.)

The *Ticonderoga* (CV-14) was commissioned in May 1944 and received an angled deck in February 1957. It then went to Alameda as its home port before leaving for Yokosuka, Japan, in September. In July 1971, it participated in the first time that an entire reserve air group (CVSGR-80) demonstrated its ability for immediate full carrier operations. This 1960s photograph shows it as CVA-14 Attack Carrier. (USN.)

Public open house days for the aircraft carriers usually included a few representative aircraft. This photograph shows a Douglas EKA-3 Skywarrior from squadron VAQ-130 on the deck of the *Oriskany* (CVA-34) at Alameda in May 1970. (WTL.)

A less common sight was a plane on exhibit on the dock next to the aircraft carrier. This Grumman E-2B Hawkeye was being viewed by the people passing by on their way to board a carrier open house in 1976. The E-2B was from VAW-113, the "Black Eagles." (WTL.)

Crew members standing on the flight deck of the *Ranger* (CVA-61) form the words "POWER FOR PEACE" as it returns to Alameda in July 1959. In September 1961, *Hancock* (CVA-19) entered the San Francisco Bay with the words "OUR TOWN" spelled out on the deck by standing sailors. (WTL.)

This scene, seldom seen by civilians, shows the crew's automobiles being transported on the flight deck of the *Enterprise* (CVN-65), and it only shows a portion of the 800 cars, as additional ones were parked on the hangar deck. Four-hundred-and-fifty crew members, and an equal number of wives and children, were aboard for the trip from Seattle to Alameda in February 1982. (WTL.)

300NE
317NE
312NE
320NE
313NE
311NE
304NE
NE

The 56,000-ton *Ranger* (CVA-61), with its sweeping 1,000-foot deck, was capable of carrying 100 aircraft. This November 4, 1967, photograph shows it leaving Alameda with Carrier Air Wing 2 bound for the western Pacific and its third Vietnam cruise. The planes on the flight deck are F-4B Phanton II fighters of VF-21 the "Free Lancers" and VF-154 "Black Knights," as well as A-4C Skyhawys of VA-22 the "Fighting Redcocks," A-7A Corsair IIs of VA-147 "Argonauts," and A-6A Intruders of VA-165 "Boomers." One RA-5C Vigilante of RVAH-6 "Fleurs" is on the bow, and the single helicopter is a UH-2C Sea Sprite of HC-1 Detachment 61 "Pacific Fleet Angels." Carrier activity at NAS Alameda has been continuous as evidenced by these escort carriers that were loading aircraft in early 1943: *Barnes* (CVE-20), *Bastian* (CVE-37), *Block Island* (CVE-21), *Bolinas* (CVE-36), *Breton* (CVE-23), *Carnegie* (CVE-38), *Cordova* (CVE-39), *Croatan* (CVE-25), *Edisto* (CVE-41), and *Glacier* (CVE-33). (WTL.)

When the carriers returned to stateside the crews were more than ready for shore leave and family reunions. This close-up of the *Enterprise* (CVN-65) bow arriving in July 1967 shows them in full dress uniform and waving at families on the Golden Gate Bridge. (WTL.)

Carriers leaving presented a far different picture of the crew in work uniforms with a sad farewell to San Francisco and the Golden Gate Bridge as the ship heads West. This is the *Ranger* (CVA-61) leaving NAS Alameda on November 16, 1972. (WTL.)

U.S. Marine Corps aircraft operating from aircraft carriers goes back to World War II. This photograph shows USMC and Navy McDonnell-Douglas F-4s on the *Enterprise* CVN-65 in June 1966. The *Coral Sea* (CVA-43) had two Marine Corps fighter squadrons (VMF-323 and VMF-531) with McDonnell-Douglas F-4Js aboard in November 1979 when it left Alameda. (WTL.)

This photograph shows a rare and unusual sight when four aircraft carriers tied up at NAS Alameda at the same time. From left to right are *Coral Sea* (CVA-43), *Hancock* (CVA-19), *Oriskany* (CVA-34), and *Enterprise* (CVA(N)-65) in 1975. (USN.)

This crowd of men, women, and children is touring the *Midway* (CV-41) during an open house in 1964 at NAS Alameda. Squadron insignias are mounted on plaques on the side of the island above the words "BEWARE PROPELLERS—JET INTAKE BLAST." (WTL.)

This *Coral Sea* (CVA-43) open house in September 1969 shows their peacetime use of lights on the carrier number in contrast with the more normal painted identification. The planes on the flight deck provided an additional exhibit for the visitors and a welcome sign said "Visitors may bring cameras on this occasion." The small, flat tugs were used to tow planes around the deck. (WTL.)

Aircraft carriers that were homeported at Alameda would hold a family day when the crew's families could come aboard and go out past the Golden Gate Bridge for a demonstration of flight operations. This graphic photograph shows the *Enterprise* (CVN-65) returning from the day's events on August 26, 1988, about to pass under the Golden Gate Bridge as it returned to Alameda. (Ronald Reuther.)

This Grumman S-3A from VS-21 is shown landing on the *Enterprise* (CVN-65) in August 1988 during flight demonstrations for the family day cruise. In addition to being able to enjoy both the hangar and flight decks, the hundreds of civilians were treated to a short demonstration of takeoffs and landings while seated in wooden bleachers built near the island. (WTL.)

Shown is a pilot's view of the USS *Carl Vinson* (CVN-70) entering the San Francisco Bay on October 7, 1995. The super carrier is over 1,000 feet long and, including the aviation complement, has a crew of over 5,600 men. The empty deck is a reminder of the change when NAS Lemoore was commissioned in 1961. Within a few years, the squadron aircraft flew from the carrier at sea to and from that air station instead of being unloaded and loaded by cranes at NAS Alameda. (WTL.)

Six

Navy and Marine Corps Reserves

In 1961, NAS Oakland closed, and its 3,000 reservists started the move to NAS Alameda with the planes flying 5 miles from Oakland Airport to NAS Alameda, followed by truck convoys through the city. Except for a break in World War II, this group operated from 1928 to 1997. In the 1980s, Naval Air Reserve Unit Alameda was the largest air reserve activity in the United States with 11 squadrons, 14 ground units, and 10 air intelligence units. In addition to Alameda, these were located at Moffett Field, Treasure Island, Monterey, Sacramento, Salt Lake City, and Hawaii. The offices were in Building 2 and the planes in Hangars 20, 21, 22, 39, and 40. (WTL.)

This Douglas A4D-1 Skyhawk shows the "6G" tail code for the Alameda Reserve Unit in July 1962. The application of both "NAVY" and "MARINES" was a short-lived indication of the use of the planes by both services. (WTL.)

By July 1968, the aircraft model designation had been changed to A-4B and the name changed to "Naval Air Reserve Training Unit" (NARTU). In April 1982, the name was changed to NAR Alameda. The Reserve Attack Squadrons at Alameda were VA-873, VA-876, and VA-879. (WTL.)

Reserve Attack Squadron VA-303, the "Golden Hawks," was stationed at Alameda from 1970 until its move to NAS Lemoore in 1984. When they transitioned from the Douglas A-4C to the Ling-Temco-Vought A-7A Corsair II in April 1971, they were the first reserve squadron in the nation to receive the A-7. This photograph shows one of their A-7As at Alameda in December 1974. In 1975, the squadron went aboard the *Ranger* (CV-61) with these planes for its annual active-duty training. (WTL.)

VA-304, the "Firebirds," was also a squadron of Carrier Air Wing Reserve Thirty (CVWR-30) flying the LTV A-7A Corsair II at Alameda in 1974. The Air Wing Reserve, consisting of nine squadrons, was established at NAS Alameda in April 1970. (WTL.)

Reserve Tactical Electronic Warfare Squadron Three Zero Eight (VAQ-308), the "Griffins," flew the Douglas KA-3B Skywarrior as shown in this May 1974 image of the reserve flight line. The squadron served aboard the *Ticonderoga* (CVS-14) overseas in Southeast Asia, at Israel during the Yom Kipper War in 1973, and during the India-Pakistan conflict. (WTL.)

Tactical Electronic Warfare Squadron Two Zero Eight (VAQ-208), the "Jockeys," also flew the Douglas KA-3B as part of Carrier Reserve Wing Twenty (CVWR-20). In August 1975, they set a record for the longest nonstop flight in a carriers-based tactical jet flying from Rota, Spain, to Alameda. This photograph was taken in the same month before the squadron was re-designated for aerial refueling. It was finally disestablished in 1989. (WTL.)

Reserve flying can be dangerous as can active duty. In this case, VAQ-308 had a fatal takeoff accident at NAS Alameda that resulted in the plane crashing into the bay in July 1977. The photograph shows the recovery operation of the KA-3B in the Oakland estuary the following day. (USN.)

Prior to the 1960s, naval reserve planes were not assigned to squadrons so they carried various names on the side (see page 100). This Grumman S-2F was unusual in having such a large identification. The tail code "7F" was changed to "6G" when the planes moved from NAS Oakland to NAS Alameda. In 1962, the reserve squadrons were renumbered and Alameda had VS-871 to VS-877. (WTL.)

Marine Reserve Squadron HMH-769, based at Alameda, flew the large Sikorsky CH-53A Sea Stallion in the 1970s. This photograph was taken in May 1975 at Treasure Island, in San Francisco Bay, with the San Francisco-Oakland Bay Bridge in the background. It was landing before giving a rappelling demonstration for the public by Marine Corps reservists. Helicopters from Alameda delivered 1,600 gallons of fresh water to Treasure Island after the 1989 earthquake. (WTL)

The Sikorsky UH-34J Seahorse was flown by Helicopter Squadrons Eight Seven One (HS-871) and Eight Seven Two (HS-872) at Alameda in the 1960s. Designed for antisubmarine warfare, the utility version deleted the ASW equipment. This photograph shows one of their UH-34Js on display at an open house in October 1965. (WTL.)

As part of an "85-Day Accelerated Recruit Training Program" in 1963, new reservists from NARTU Alameda joined others from NAS Los Alamitos and NAS Seattle for five days at sea on the *Midway*. Additional training included a week at Treasure Island and two weeks in various NAS Alameda shops. (USN.)

Although the navy had a number of the two-place Lockheed TV-2 trainers, the same aircraft as the U.S. Air Force T-33A, and although the navy had 698 of them, they were a rare sight in the naval reserve. NAS Alameda had one, as can be seen by this photograph of bureau No. 143025 in July 1962. With the DOD designation change in September 1962 it became a T-33B. (WTL.)

Aircraft from reserve units around the United States visited Alameda on cross-country training flights. This Fairchild C-119F (formerly R4Q-2) is from the Marine Corps Reserve at Seattle (7T) and was photographed at Alameda in October 1965. (WTL.)

When this photograph was taken in July 1962 of VS-872s Grumman S2F-1, the squadron had been called to active duty as can be seen by the tail code "SW." Within three months, the aircraft designation for the S2F Tracker changed to S-2 as part of the Department of Defense consolidation of the U.S. Air Force and U.S. Navy model designations into one system. (WTL.)

Although most of the Lockheed P2V Neptunes in the Alameda Reserve were P2V-5s, there was at least one P2V-6, as shown in this photograph of BuNo 126533 in July 1962. The Dash-6 model was modified for aerial mine laying with guns in the nose that have been removed at this time. (WTL.)

The change in the tail code from "6G" to "PS" is an indication that this Lockheed P2V-5F Neptune is an active-duty squadron. Patrol Squadron Eight Seven Two (VP-872) was activated in October 1961 and released back to the reserves in August 1962. See the photograph of the commanding officer on page 110. (WTL.)

6G
6G
203
NAVY
NAVY
2773
ATD MARCH 1962 VP-874

This formal portrait of the officers and enlisted men and women of Patrol Squadron Eight Seven Four (VP-874) was taken in March 1962 when they were called to temporary active duty. The Lockheed P2V Neptunes lined up with their Alameda tail code of "6G" are 203, 201, and 205. NARTU Alameda was also the home of VP-871, VP-872, VP-873, VP-875, VP-876, and VP-878. (USN.)

In August 1962, Fleet Admiral Chester Nimitz reviewed the officers and men from three reserve squadrons returning from active duty. Capt. Raymond E. Hill, commanding officer of the Naval Aviation Reserve Training Unit at Alameda, is to his left. Note the three press photographers disrupting the formal ceremony. (USN.)

From left to right are Comdr. Edward Roberts (CO of VP-872), Capt. Raymond Hill (CO NARTU Alameda), Fleet Admiral Chester Nimitz, Comdr. William Worden (CO VS-872), and Comdr. Robert Mini (CO VS-873).

Seven

BASE CLOSURE AND MUSEUM

The Alameda Naval Air Museum is dedicated to preserving the rich history of NAS Alameda, and volunteers maintain exhibits and a library on three floors of the original air terminal, now Building 77 on Ferry Point Street. In addition to providing an educational experience about the air station for visitors and students, the museum is a resource for information and research about naval aviation in the Pacific. The museum maintains an excellent Web site with extensive information at alamedanavalairmuseum.org, combining historical data and photographs with current information. Further information and museum photographs can be seen at ebdir.net/vsf1/nas_museum.html. (WTL.)

The USS *Hornet* (CVS-12) is now a floating museum berthed at Pier 3, 707 West Hornet Avenue, Alameda Point. Because of the hours of volunteer work, the ship is open for guided tours or individual exploration with many exhibits. Private events are held as well as special ones such as the New Year's Eve dance and dinner for 1,200 people. The carrier's involvement with the Apollo 11 Space Program is covered by extensive exhibits, as well as 11 aircraft carrier memorial compartments. The museum has a Web site at uss-hornet.org with full information. The "Doolittle Raiders," after loading 16 B-25s aboard the *Hornet* (CV-8), left Alameda on April 2, 1942, for their famous attack on Japan. (WTL.)

The *Hornet*, once considered a "large aircraft carrier," is now surrounded by the Maritime Administration Ready Reserve Fleet at Piers 1, 2, and 3, as can be seen in this 2004 photograph. The blurred image in the bottom portion was caused by the curved, double-pane window in a Southwest Airways Boeing 737. (WTL.)

One of the aircraft displayed on the *Hornet* (CVS-12) is this F8U-1 Crusader with the markings of VF-154 when it was aboard the *Coral Sea* (CVA-43) in 1965. Others are a TA-4J, F-14A, FJ-2, S-3, US-2B, T-28B, TBM-3, HUP-1, SH-2, SH-3H, and UH-34D. (WTL.)

The former reserve Hangar 21 is now the home of St. George Spirits Distillery at 2601 Monarch Street. The hangar now provides the storage and shipping activities generated by a new 1,000-liter still. (WTL.)

The remains of Reserve Attack Squadron Three Zero Four (VA-304) "WELCOME FROM THE FIREBIRDS" sign remains on their hangar in 2009. The squadron was disestablished in December 1994 before the closure of NAS Alameda. (WTL.)

The operations building and control tower have been reconditioned and are now, in 2009, being used by Alameda Point Community Partners (the selected master developer of Alameda Point) and a wind-power research development company. (WTL.)

The salute guns at the control tower, which took part in so many important ceremonies welcoming admirals and other VIPs, stand silent today. The Alameda Naval Air Museum is requesting one from the navy to be placed in front of Building 77 as a permanent reminder of their active years at the air station. (WTL.)

The former WAVE barracks are in a serious deteriorating condition, which is an alarm to those who would like to save at least one as a historic item, even as a historic monument, for future Alameda Point residents and visitors. (WTL.)

While some buildings, such as this one, are in poor condition, others have been rehabilitated and are in use by such companies as Area 51 Productions, Delphi Productions, Event Productions, Hesco, Pacific Fine Food Catering, Protector USA, and West Coast Novelty. (WTL.)

Only birds now land on Runway 25, but the tire marks remind one of an active past. It was used in 1998 for the electric car show and in 2003 for the filming of the freeway chase scene in the movie *Matrix Reloaded*. This view is looking west toward San Francisco. (Tim Tyler.)

Many large building complexes such as this one are scheduled for demolition to make way for new structures in the overall planning process for Alameda Point. Others, such as Nelson's marine boatyard and maintenance/restoration facility near the USS Hornet Museum, will remain and may include 600 private boat slips if present planning becomes reality. (WTL.)

The large munition storage facility that included "special weapons" was far out to the west away from the main base. It was officially designated as an "Earth Covered High Explosives Standard Igloo." (Tim Tyler.)

Thousands of civilian employees, as well as navy personnel, worked at NAS Alameda for years but never saw this view of one of the ammunition storage areas on the west end of the air station. NADEP added a gun repair and test facility in 1989. (Tim Tyler.)

The large 63,000-square-foot paint and finishing facility was completed in 1991. It has two Lockheed P-3–sized hangar bays and one Grumman A-6–sized bay for components painting and aircraft conversion coating and painting. It has a water deluge fire protection system, air pollution controlled ventilation, and an independent industrial waste treatment plant. (WTL.)

This 2009 photograph of the Seaplane Lagoon, with the seaplane hangars in the distant background, appears so beautiful that it clashes with the environmental issues raised by the navy's report that 300 million gallons of industrial wastewater—containing heavy metals, solvents, paints, detergents, acids, caustics, mercury, oil, grease, and radium—were dumped into it. The concern is so severe that there is a ban on disturbing the mud and silt on the bottom of the lagoon. (WTL.)

A California historical landmark plaque in front of Building 1 reads, "Site of the China Clipper Flight Departure—Pan American Airways' fabled China Clipper (Martin M/130 Flying Boat) left Alameda Marina on November 22, 1935. Under the command of Captain Edwin C. Musick, the flight would reach Manila via Honolulu, Midway, Wake, and Guam. The inauguration of ocean airmail service and commercial air flight across the Pacific was a significant event for both California and the world." (WTL.)

This 2009 view of the West Essex Drive side of the large Bachelors Officers Quarters (BOQ) shows just one part of the now empty complex. (WTL.)

Another 2009 view looking east toward West Tower Avenue and Monarch Street shows the new Alameda Point activity. The end of the Seaplane Hangar Row is on the right, and Building 5 on the left is part of the former NARF/NADEP overhaul facility. (WTL.)

The continuing problem of the toxic cleanup of Alameda Point was escalated in the summer of 2009, when additional radioactive contamination was found in the vicinity of Buildings 5 and 400, resulting in a large area being closed off as shown in this photograph at West Tower and Monarch Streets. Investigation and remediation was started in 1998 and continues with concerns of the Seaplane Lagoon as well as other places on the air station. The disagreement over how much of the cleanup will be paid for by the navy and how much by the city remains an active concern of both the City of Alameda and its residents. (WTL.)

This Douglas A-4C Skyhawk has seven lives and is being carefully restored from the windstorm damage that toppled it from its pedestal. A small crew of dedicated volunteers is devoting many hours to fabricating and installing damaged parts, as shown in this 2009 photograph. When that work is completed, it will be mounted again inside the main gate between Second and Third Streets. (WTL.)

The Vought A-7A Corsair II has weathered storms and the base closure in better condition, and this 2009 photograph shows it still mounted on its pylon on Atlantic Avenue inside the east gate. It now carries the insignia of Reserve Squadron VA-304 "Firebirds" on the tail. (WTL.)

Exhibits honoring the history of naval aviation, as well as operations in the Pacific, fill the first floor of the Alameda Naval Air Museum. This particular exhibit covers the December 7, 1941, attack on Pearl Harbor. The museum has a small theater and a gift shop. (WTL.)

Uniforms, ship models, and other exhibits give a broad picture of the U.S. Navy. A large exhibit of aircraft models fills a portion of the second floor of the museum. Pan American Airways operations at Alameda are also presented in a special exhibit. (WTL.)

The museum book committee at a preliminary meeting in 2008 shows, from left to right, Marilyn York (president of the Alameda Naval Air Museum), William Larkins, David Balmer, Larry Pirack, Devon Weston, Bronson Parry, and Barbara Baack. Kin Robles is not shown, as he was kind enough to take the photograph. (Kinden Robles.)

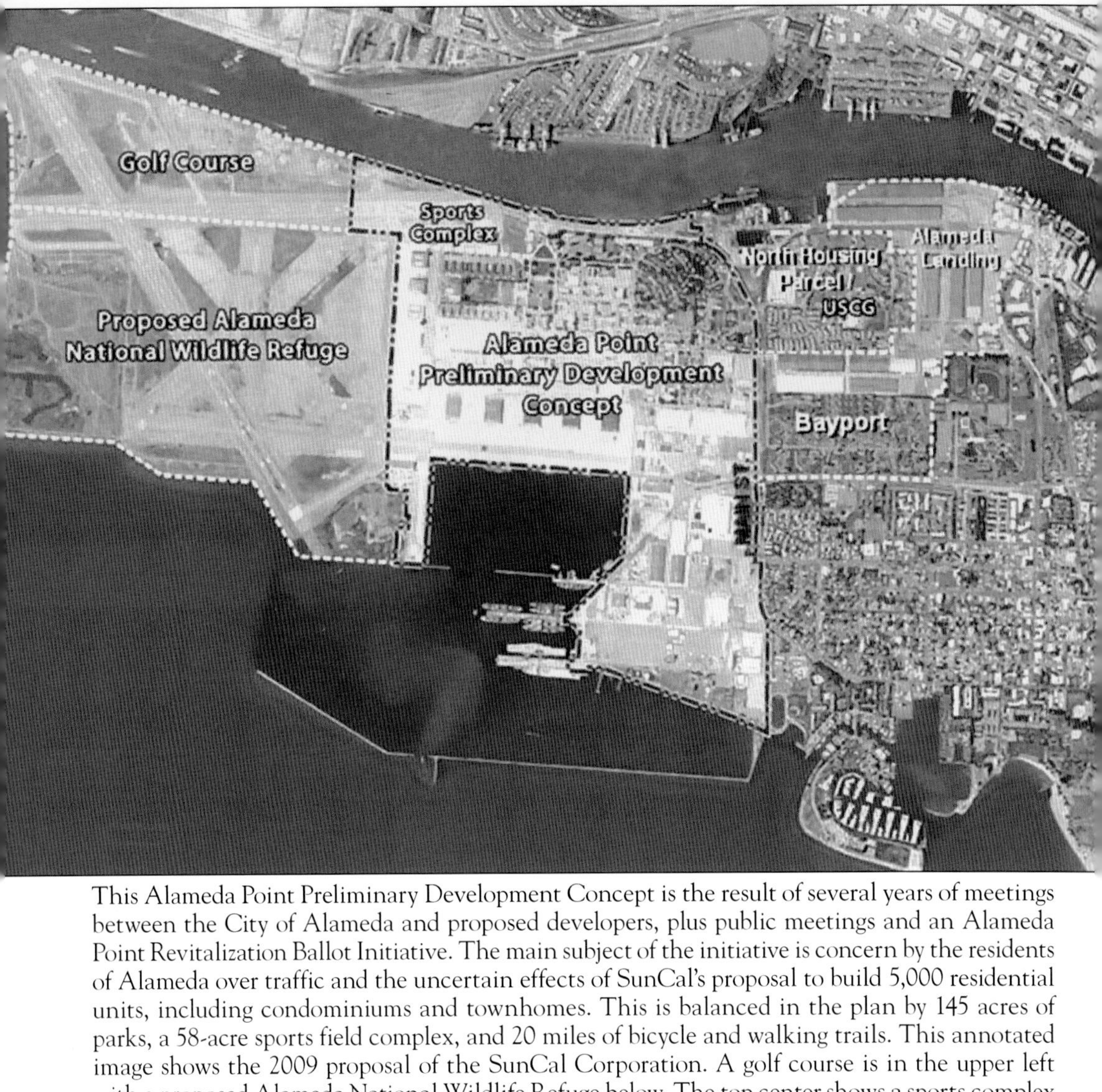

This Alameda Point Preliminary Development Concept is the result of several years of meetings between the City of Alameda and proposed developers, plus public meetings and an Alameda Point Revitalization Ballot Initiative. The main subject of the initiative is concern by the residents of Alameda over traffic and the uncertain effects of SunCal's proposal to build 5,000 residential units, including condominiums and townhomes. This is balanced in the plan by 145 acres of parks, a 58-acre sports field complex, and 20 miles of bicycle and walking trails. This annotated image shows the 2009 proposal of the SunCal Corporation. A golf course is in the upper left with a proposed Alameda National Wildlife Refuge below. The top center shows a sports complex and below it the current land and buildings of NAS Alameda. The Alameda Landing and U.S. Coast Guard housing in the upper right are on property outside of the air station. Bayport, in the right center, is the first new development at Alameda Point. The 2003 Reuse Plan establishing guidelines for the development of the area extends to the year 2020. (City of Alameda.)

The former administration structure, Building 1 at C and Second Streets, has been saved, cleaned, and painted and is now an active Alameda City Hall West. Once the center of activity on the air station, it now faces an empty but well-kept parade ground. Alameda City Public Works Department is also at Alameda Point. (WTL.)

Some of the original street signs on the air station have been replaced with new green ones sporting the Alameda City logo as part of the rehabilitation to become Alameda Point. This is the intersection of Pan Am Way (Pan American Airways) and Sunrise Court. (WTL.)